BEHIND THE SCENES

FASHION

Frances Ridley

Editorial Consultant – Cliff Moon

RISING STARS
Schools Library and Infomation Services

S00000689738

nasen
NASEN House, 4/5 Amber Business Village, Amber Close,
Amington, Tamworth, Staffordshire B77 4RP

Rising Stars UK Ltd.
22 Grafton Street, London W1S 4EX
www.risingstars-uk.com

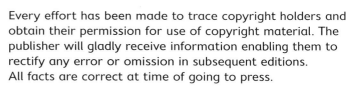

Every effort has been made to trace copyright holders and
obtain their permission for use of copyright material. The
publisher will gladly receive information enabling them to
rectify any error or omission in subsequent editions.
All facts are correct at time of going to press.

First published 2006

Cover design: Button plc
Cover image: Alamy
Illustrator: Bill Greenhead
Text design and typesetting: Marmalade Book Design
(www.marmaladebookdesign.com)
Educational consultants: Cliff Moon, Lorraine Petersen and
Paul Blum
Technical consultant: Gaynor Spry
Pictures: The Advertising Archives: pages 21, 37
Alamy: pages 4, 9, 12, 21, 23, 26, 27, 30, 31, 42-43, 46
Empics: pages 6, 7, 8, 9, 13, 16, 24, 29, 30, 39, 40, 41
Getty Images: pages 14, 15, 25, 36, 39
howies: page 28
THTC/Designer: mau-mau.co.uk: page 29

British Library Cataloguing in Publication Data.
A CIP record for this book is available from the British
Library.

ISBN: 978-1-84680- 044-3

Printed by Craftprint International Ltd., Singapore

Contents

Fashion brands 4

Fashion trends 6

High-street fashion 8

Retro Rocks – Part one 10

Urban clothing 12

    Hip-hop brands 14

    Cashing in on urban style 16

Retro Rocks – Part two 18

Sportswear 20

    History of a brand: Nike 22

Fashion issues 26

Eco-chic 28

Vintage clothing 30

    Retro labels 31

Retro Rocks – Part three 32

History of a brand: Diesel 36

Designer labels 40

Fashion shows 42

Quiz 44

Glossary of terms 45

More resources 46

Answers 47

Index 48

Fashion brands

Fashion is a huge business.

There are lots of different clothes to choose from.

Some people wear the latest fashions.

Some people wear fashions to do with music or sport.

Other people wear clothes that show what they think.

Each fashion brand aims its clothes at a **target market**.

It has to work out what this market wants.

Target market

How much money does he have?

How old is he?

What does he like to do?

What does he think is important?

Fashion trends

Fashions change all the time and fashion brands have to keep up.

Some fashion trends start on the **catwalk**.

Other fashion trends start on the street.

Anything can start a new trend – a new film, a new band or a new idea.

Kate Moss has started trends with the clothes she wears.

Coolhunters go out on to the streets and into clubs.

They look at what people are wearing.

They find out what people are into.

They talk to people who look cool.

Coolhunters use the information to **predict** new trends.

Sports can also influence trends.

High-street fashion

There are many fashion brands on the high street. They find different ways to get noticed!

H&M is famous for its **advertising campaigns**.

It asked Stella McCartney to design a **clothing line**.

When the Stella range went on sale, stores around the world sold out of stock within an hour!

Zara doesn't have **advertising campaigns**.

Its large, smart shops are its advertisements!

TopMan has made strong links with the music business. It says: 'Music is what boys are interested in.'

TopMan **sponsored** the **NME**'s Best Dressed Award in 2005.

Brandon Flowers from The Killers won.

Retro Rocks (Part one)

"Look at that!" said Jez with a sneer.

A girl went past their table.

"She looks OK," said Tom.

"Yeah, right," said Jez. "She's wearing a jumper her gran made!"

Tom looked at Kim. They didn't say anything.

"Anyway," said Jez. "Got to go. See you later."

"Jez always goes on about how people look," said Tom.

"It's because his dad has a clothes shop,"
said Kim.

"Yeah," said Tom. "Everything he wears has
a label on it. I can't even afford a cap like his!"

Kim grinned.

"Do you *want* a cap like his? It's alright –
but it's not interesting!"

She finished her drink. Tom still looked fed up.

"You need to meet Lara," said Kim.

"Who's Lara?" asked Tom.

"The coolest person I know," said Kim.

Continued on page 18

11

Urban clothing

Some people who listen to hip-hop music wear urban clothing.

Urban fashion has changed over the years – but jeans, '**kicks**' and **accessories** have always been part of the look.

Hip-hop **accessories**

Baseball cap

Do-rag

Chains

Hip-hop fashion likes to put its wealth on show. Expensive jewellery and the right brands are part of the look. It's cool to leave price tags showing.

P Diddy is a singer and a music producer. He has his own **clothing line** called 'Sean Jean' and loves hip-hop fashion and jewellery.

Hip-hop brands

Many hip-hop brands were started by hip-hop musicians.

RocaWear was started by Damon Dash and Jay-Z. They head the Roc-a-Fella label.

Phat Farm was started by Russell Simmons, from Def Jam. His wife also runs the fashion label, Baby Phat.

Akademiks was started by Donwan Harrell. He used to be a top designer at Nike. Akademiks make PRPS jeans on Levi's looms from the 1960s. David Beckham wears PRPS jeans.

Cashing in on urban style

Urban style started on the street, but it has become big business. Sports brands have a close link with hip hop.

Adidas teamed up with Missy Elliott in 2004. They produced the 'Respect ME' **clothing line**.

Fashion facts!

Russell Simmons sold Phat farm for $140 million in 2004.

R 'n' B singer Cassie promoted 'Respect ME' clothes.

Logo trouble!

Missy Elliott designed the logo for 'Respect ME'.

The Queen of Denmark complained that
the logo copied her royal **monogram**!

Retro Rocks (Part two)

Next Saturday, Kim took Tom and Jez to Lara's shop – Retro Rocks.

It sold vintage clothes and jewellery. Kim tried on a necklace and earrings – they looked great!

"I make the jewellery," said Lara, "with junk and imagination!"

"And people wear this stuff?" gasped Jez.

Tom and Kim loved the shop. It was really different! Tom got a T-shirt and Kim got a dress. Jez didn't get anything.

"Thanks for coming," said Lara. "These are for you." She gave Tom and Kim a necklace each.

"What will I do with a necklace?" asked Tom.

"Use your imagination!" said Lara.

Tom grinned. He twisted the necklace round his wrist, twice.

"You look stupid," said Jez.

"Maybe I do," said Tom. "But at least I look interesting!"

Continued on page 32

Sportswear

Sportswear has to:

- perform well in sport

- look good.

Most sports brands try to balance **function** with fashion.

Function

David Beckham wore these Adidas boots in the 2006 Football World Cup. Each boot shows five lions. The total of ten lions stands for each of Beckham's team mates!

Fashion

Stella McCartney designed these Adidas clothes.

The football hero Pelé starred in this Puma advert. It was made for the 2006 Football World Cup.

Fashion fact!

Adidas and Puma were started by two brothers. The two companies are fierce rivals!

History of a brand: Nike

1960s

Phil Knight and Bill Bowerman start 'Blue Ribbon Sports'. They sell running shoes made in Japan.

Bowerman wants to make a light shoe with good grip. He pours rubber into a **waffle iron**. The **waffle iron** is ruined – but Bowerman has a sole for his shoe! The company starts making its own shoes.

Knight pays a student to design a logo for the shoeboxes. The result is the 'swoosh'. It's a perfect brand logo – simple yet strong.

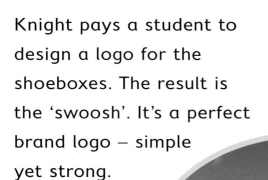

The 'swoosh' can be used on any product or place.

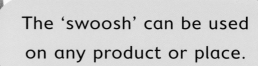

1970s

The company changes its name to Nike. Nike is the name of the Greek goddess of victory.

1980s

Nike signs up basketball player Michael Jordan to **endorse** its products. Nike's 'Air Jordans' become a best-seller. They are sports shoes – and fashion items! Jordan stars in advertisements with the slogan 'Just do it!' Nike becomes a **global** brand.

1990s

Newspapers report on Nike's factories. They say Nike pays low wages to its workers and then sells its shoes for high prices. Nike works hard to clean up its act.

2000s

Nike is still the strongest sportswear brand.

Nike paid 18-year-old basketball star LeBron James $90 million to **endorse** its products!

Fashion issues

Many clothes are made in **developing countries** because it is cheaper and faster to make clothes there.

Some factory workers are treated badly.

They work long hours and are not paid much money.

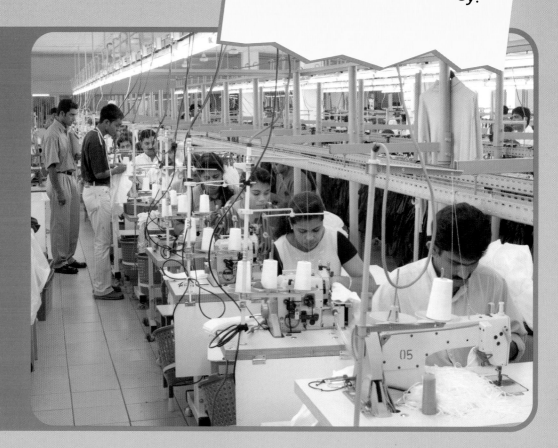

Many clothes are made from cotton.

A lot of cotton is grown in **developing countries**.

Many farmers don't get a fair price for their cotton.

Many cotton growers use a lot of chemicals.

Cotton also needs a lot of water when it is growing.

Both these things harm the planet.

Eco-chic

Eco-chic brands:

- use **organic** cotton

- pay a fair price for cotton

- pay factory workers a fair wage

- don't make workers work long hours.

Howies clothes are popular with bikers and skaters.

THTC clothes are popular with hip-hop fans. They describe their clothes as 'urban eco-wear'.

Edun was set up by Ali Hewson. Hewson is married to Bono from U2.

Edun wants to help **developing countries** with trade, not aid.

Vintage clothing

'Retro' means clothes that are old or look old.

Vintage clothing is good-quality second-hand clothing. You can look cool, recycle and save money all at the same time!

Fashion fact!

Julia Roberts wore a vintage gown when she won an Oscar!

ALL OF OUR VINTAGE FURS ARE MOSTLY FROM THE 1960s

ALL UNDER £75

The Portobello Road market in London is a good place to look for vintage clothes.

New vintage

Many fashion labels have a 'vintage' line.
The clothes are new, but they look old.

Hugo Boss and Gap make vintage jeans and T-shirts. Shops like Urban Outfitters sell 'new vintage' clothing.

Retro labels

Some retro labels have been making the same products for many years.

Converse All-Stars have been made since 1917.

Retro Rocks (Part three)

Kim, Tom and Jez went to a café near the shop.

As soon as they sat down, Jez started.

"Look at *her*!" he said with a sneer.

Kim looked. There was a woman wearing
a funky outfit.

"I think she looks cool," Kim said.

The woman got up to pay. On her way over,
she stopped at their table.

"Hi," she said to Tom. "I'm Rosie. I've been
looking at your wristband. It's cool. Where did
you get it?"

"Retro Rocks," said Tom. "It's a shop just over
there. We're friends with the owner, Lara."

"That's great!" said Rosie. She sat down.

Continued on the next page

"I'd like to meet Lara," said Rosie. "I'm a cool-hunter. I look out for fashion trends. Lara's on to something with this wristband idea. Tell her to call this number if she's interested."

Rosie passed a card to Kim. Then she got up to go, but Jez stopped her.

"Wait!" he said. "My dad owns a clothes shop too!"

Rosie looked him up and down. "Really?" she said. "That's nice."

"Well," said Jez. "Don't you want to give me a card?"

"Sorry," said Rosie. "I look for new and interesting fashion trends. Your clothes are fine – but they're not different from anybody else's."

Rosie left the café. Jez looked disgusted.

"You look like you're chewing a wasp," said Kim.

"No," said Jez. "I guess she's right, but I think the wasp just chewed me!"

History of a brand: Diesel

Diesel is an Italian company. It was started by Renzo Rosso.

Diesel sells clothes that look 'vintage'. It sees itself as 'anti-fashion'.

Rosso's rule for life is: 'Be true to yourself and your ideas.'

Diesel is famous for its jeans.

It is also famous for its advertising.

Diesel's adverts always have a twist – this looks like an advert for smoking, but it has a strong anti-smoking message.

1960s

Renzo Rosso is 15. He makes jeans on his mum's sewing machine and sells them to his friends.

1978

Rosso starts the 'Diesel' jeans label with a partner. The word is used all over the world and every country says it the same way!

DIESEL ®

JEANS AND WORKWEAR

1985

Rosso buys out his business partner. He loves vintage denim and makes jeans that look old. The shops send them back! At last, Rosso gets a small space in a New York vintage store. The jeans sell out instantly!

1990s

Diesel starts marketing across the world.
It opens its first **flagship store** in New York. Diesel becomes a major label in the fashion world.

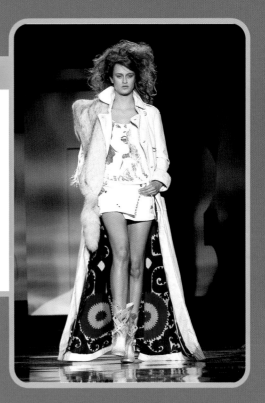

2000s

Today, Diesel sells its clothes in more than 80 countries.

Designer labels

Designer clothing is made by top designers.

Most designer clothing is very expensive.

Hedi Slimane is famous for his narrow black suits.

Stars such as Alex Kapranos, Brad Pitt and Will Smith wear his clothes.

Ozwald Boateng also makes suits.

He is famous for his use of bright colour.

He has designed suits for the James Bond films.

John Galliano

John Galliano works for the famous fashion brand Dior.

He loves to shock the fashion world. He always wears an unusual outfit at the end of each show!

Fashion shows

Designers plan and make **collections** of clothes. The **collections** are shown at fashion shows.

Fashion shows are held all over the world. The most famous shows are in Paris, New York, London and Milan.

Fashion facts!

Catwalk shows are important. They get fashion into the **media**.

Designers spend thousands of pounds to put on a good show.

The clothes are shown on a **catwalk** that goes right into the audience.

The audience can see the clothes from every angle.

Quiz

1   Which famous designer designed a clothing line for H&M?

2   What is the hip-hop word for trainers?

3   Which famous jeans label does Akademiks make?

4   Who designed the 'Respect ME' logo?

5   What did Nike used to be called?

6   What was Nike's famous 1980s slogan?

7   Who is married to the creator of the Edun label?

8   Where did Diesel open its first flagship store?

9   What is Hedi Slimane famous for?

10 Where are the most famous fashion shows held?

Glossary of terms

accessories
Things that go with an outfit – like jewellery or a hat.

advertising campaign
A plan to sell a product through the media.

catwalk
A long platform that models walk up and down to show off clothes.

clothing line
A group of clothes that have something in common.

collections
Clothes that have been designed together as a group.

developing countries
Poorer countries that are trying to become richer.

endorse
Say that you like or use something.

flagship store
A company's most important store.

function
The way something is used.

global
All over the world.

kicks
The hip-hop word for trainers.

media
Television, radio, magazines and the Internet.

monogram
A logo made up of two letters.

organic
Grown without using chemicals.

predict
Say what is going to happen.

sponsor
Give money to someone in return for them advertising your product.

target market
The people to whom you want to sell.

waffle iron
A tool for making waffles with – it gets very hot.

More resources

Books

Sneakers: The Complete Collectors' Guide
Publisher: Thames & Hudson Ltd.
ISBN: 0500512159
180 sneaker designs from 11 leading brands!

100% Cotton: T-shirt Graphics
Publisher: Watson-Guptill Publications
ISBN: 0823033554
Lots of T-shirt designs with notes on the history of T-shirts and why we love wearing them!

Magazines

GQ
Condé Nast

Information about fashion and style, as well as music, film and news.

Websites

www.GQStyle.com
Pictures of the latest designer collections and information about new fashion trends.

These two sites sell eco-friendly clothing:
www.howies.co.uk
www.thtc.co.uk

www.asos.com
If your favourite celebrity has worn something you like, you'll probably be able to buy it from here.

DVDs

Zoolander (2001)
Paramount Home Entertainment (Cat. No. PHE8166)
Comedy about male supermodels.

Answers

1 Stella McCartney

2 Kicks

3 PRPS

4 Missy Elliott

5 Blue Ribbon Sports

6 Just do it!

7 Bono

8 New York

9 Narrow black suits

10 Paris, New York, London and Milan

Index

Adidas   16, 20, 21

Advertisement   8, 9, 21, 24, 37

Akademiks   15

Baby Phat   15

Beckham, David   15, 20

Blue Ribbon Sports   22

Boateng, Ozwald   41

Bowerman, Bill   22-25

Brand4-5, 6, 8-9, 13, 14-15, 16, 20,
            22-25, 28-29, 36-39, 41

Catwalk   6, 42-43

Converse All-Stars   31

Coolhunter   7

Cotton industry   27-28

Dash, Damon   14

Def Jam   15

Design   8, 17, 20, 23, 40-41

Designer   8, 15, 20, 40-41, 42-43

Diddy, P   13

Diesel   36-39

Eco-chic   28-29

Edun   29

Elliott, Missy   16-17

Factories   25, 26, 28

Fashion show   42-43

Flowers, Brandon   9

Football World Cup   20-21

Galliano, John   41

H&M   8

Harrell, Donwan   15

Hewson, Ali   29

Hip-hop   12-16, 29

Howies   28

James, LeBron   25

Jay-Z   14

Jeans   12, 15, 31, 36, 38-9

Jordan, Michael   24

Knight, Phil   22-25

Label   14, 15, 31, 39, 40-41

Levi's   15

Logo   17, 23

McCartney, Stella   8, 20

Moss, Kate   6

Music   4, 6, 9, 12-17

New York   38, 39, 42

NME   9

Pelé   21

Phat Farm   15, 16

Puma   21

'Respect ME'   16-17

Roberts, Julia   30

Roc-a-Fella   14

RocaWear   14

Rosso, Renzo   36, 38-39

'Sean Jean'   13

Simmons, Russell   15, 16

Slimane, Hedi   40

Slogan   24

Sport   4, 7, 16, 20-21, 24, 25

Sportswear   20-21, 22-25

THTC   29

TopMan   9

Trend   6-7

Urban fashion   12-17

Urban Outfitters   31

Vintage   30-31, 36, 38

Zara   9